# How Not To Die

## *50 Whole Food, Budget Friendly Meals*

## Reduce Your Meat Intake And Embrace A Plant Based Diet To Prevent Long-Term Health Implications

# By: Anthony Wynne

# Table Of Contents

# Introduction

Do you want to live a long life? Then you must start following the Whole Food, Plant Based Diet as soon as possible!

Time has tested and proven the fact that those who eat a diet rich in fruits, vegetables, nuts, seeds, whole grains, legumes, and tubers inevitably live longer than those who live on a diet made up primarily of meat and other animal products. By choosing to follow a plant based diet, you are helping your body become stronger, more resistant to illness and long-term diseases, and look better to boot!

This book will let you know why the whole food, plant based diet is the best diet for your health. It will also teach you how to prepare fifty easy, affordable, and delicious whole food, plant based dishes at home. Build weeks' worth of meal plans by mixing and matching breakfast, soup, salad, main dish, and side dish recipes in this book.

If you are someone who wants to live long and look good at the same time, then this book is definitely meant for you!

# Chapter 1 - The Whole Food Plant Based Diet

Who would not want to make the most out of their lives? There is so much that the world can offer to someone who has big goals and amazing ideas. But one crucial factor plays a role in determining how and when you can see your goals turn into a reality, and that is your health.

No matter how hardworking and inspired you are, everything will come tumbling down once your health suffers. Fortunately, you can help your body slow down the aging process and boost its immune system by eating a diet that is plant based and composed of whole food.

## What is the Whole Food Plant Based Diet?

This diet is one that focuses on the consumption of whole (meaning unrefined) edible plants, or fruits, vegetables, whole grains, legumes, and tubers. What makes it different from a vegetarian or vegan diet is it does not really speak against the consumption of eggs, dairy products, and meat, but it does discourage it. It also advised against eating refined sugar, oils, and bleached flour.

One wrong assumption about this diet is that it concentrates mainly on vegetables. On the contrary, it does not want you to eat leafy greens alone every day for the rest of your life. Instead, it is about eating a variety of whole foods so that your body would be able to obtain the different nutrients from each food, and not just a certain nutrient from one health plant.

Another misconception about this diet is that it does not allow starch-based food when in fact, the foundation of this diet is healthy starches. Nowadays, there is a negative perception of tubers such as potatoes, corn, brown rice, and legumes such as garbanzo beans (chickpeas).

However, the truth is that they are only unhealthy when they are drenched in dairy products and oil. By preparing them in another way, such as through baking and steaming, they are just as healthy and nutritious as any other edible plant. Furthermore, they can help make you feel satisfied for longer periods of time.

All in all, the whole food plant based diet is about eating a wide variety of unprocessed or minimally processed food (such as frozen whole foods) to give your body all the nutrients that it needs to keep the different demands of its parts healthy. It is understandable that there is no such food that contains all of the nutrients your body needs, that is why variety is of the essence.

## What are the Health Benefits of Eating a Whole Food Plant Based Diet?

Truth be told, most human beings eat too much meat and other animal products. What is worse, these are prepared in the least healthy ways, such as by adding preservatives, by deep frying and by coating with artificial flavorings. They are also often paired with equally unhealthy side dishes, such as processed starchy vegetables soaked in high fat, high sugar sauces.

If you have been eating a primarily meat-based diet and are experiencing health problems left and right, then you absolutely must transition to the whole food plant based diet if you want to live a longer life. There are so many health benefits that await you when you commit to this diet:

### *Reduced Bad Cholesterol*

Bad cholesterol inevitably leads to heart disease. It is a term that is often mentioned in hospitals, in fact, because it is one of the things that doctors constantly point to as the culprit to many heart conditions. Plants have absolutely no bad cholesterol, because this can only be obtained from meat products and other animal by-products. Eggs, for instance, are chock full of cholesterol. The only way to reduce your bad cholesterol levels is to get rid of meat and animal by-products from your diet and to start eating plants.

### Decreased Blood Pressure

Unhealthy fats and cholesterol from a high fat, meat-based, processed food diet will choke your arteries and lead to heart attacks, stroke, and lethal cardiovascular diseases. A person who is suffering from high blood pressure is also more likely to experience these symptoms every time they feel anxiety and stress. Two important nutrients found in a plant based diet that is greatly lacking in a meat based one are vitamin B6 and potassium, and they are what can help you reduce blood pressure.

### Healthy Blood Sugar Levels

Diabetes is the silent killer because it increases your bad cholesterol, blood sugar, and blood pressure levels constantly, leading to a slow but deadly breakdown of all your bodily functions. The best way to help bring your blood sugar levels back to normal is by eating more fiber. This is because it helps your digestive system absorb sugars at a much slower rate. Leafy greens and other high fiber plants in your diet, therefore, are the solution.

### Lower Risk of Developing Cancer

Consumption of meat is scientifically proven to trigger the growth of cancer-causing cells in the body. A plant based diet is the exact opposite of this, as many plants are rich in antioxidants that can help your body fight off the growth of cancer cells, particularly for colon cancer.

## *Weight Loss*

Weight loss is one of the health benefits that dieters want to see simply because it is one change that you can easily observe when you are standing in front of the mirror. A whole food plant based diet will easily let you lose weight simply because it is high in nutrients and fiber and low in calories. In other words, you are not going to be hungry as frequently throughout the day and your body will have the nutrients it needs to get things done throughout the day without your constant need to eat something.

There are plenty of other health benefits once you stick to the whole food plant based diet. Many people experience other wonderful changes, such as having healthier hair, clear skin, stronger nails, better energy, and more concentration.

## How to Maintain a Kitchen for the Whole Food Plant Based Diet

It is difficult to eat healthy when you do not prepare your own food because of two things: one, healthy meals are more expensive when bought in a restaurant or even for take-out; and two, there are too few healthy restaurants in the first place.

To make this diet sustainable for you and your family, you must make your home, specifically your kitchen, conducive for it. Here are some tips to help you:

❖ Clear out your kitchen of any foods that do not adhere to the diet, such as processed food, junk food, and so on.

❖ Supply your kitchen with tools and equipment commonly used to prepare plant based meals. Buy the high quality kind and keep these in full display to encourage yourself to use them as often as possible. The most useful ones are: extra sharp knives, chopping boards, a mandolin, a vegetable peeler, a colander, a salad spinner, mixing bowls, a food processor, a spiralizer (to make noodles out of zucchinis and so on), a steamer, a wok, a citrus juicer, a grater, a mortar and pestle, and a zester.

❖ Stock up on herbs and spices. If you are new to the diet, you can start with the dried herbs and spices, but as time goes on you will find it to be more economical to grow your own. Start a little herb and spice garden on your windowsill or backyard. Your health and wallet will thank you.

❖ Keep a list of the fruits, vegetables, and other whole food produce that are seasonal and locally available in your market. Talk to

13

your local farmers to learn about this or visit your local garden center to get some information. It is a priority to eat whatever is organic, in-season, and locally produced in this diet.

# Chapter 2 - Breakfast

## *Mason Jar Overnight Oatmeal*
*Makes 2 servings*

### Ingredients

- ❖ 1 cup steel-cut oats
- ❖ 2 bananas
- ❖ 1 cup pure coconut milk
- ❖ 2 tsp pure maple syrup
- ❖ 2 tsp dried berries of any kind
- ❖ 2 tsp almonds or Brazil nuts
- ❖ 2 Tbsp ground flax seeds
- ❖ 1 Tbsp almond butter
- ❖ Cinnamon

### How to Prepare

1. Combine the nuts, almond butter, coconut milk, maple syrup, and bananas in a blender or food processor. Add a generous dash of cinnamon. Process until smooth.

2. Fold in the oats and flax seeds, then pour into two small sterilized mason jars. Spoon the dried berries and nuts on top of each serving, then seal.

3. Refrigerate overnight and serve chilled the following morning.

# *Tofu Frittata*

*Makes 3 servings*

## Ingredients

- ❖ 1/2 lb extra firm tofu, drained thoroughly

- ❖ 3/4 tsp Dijon mustard

- ❖ 1/2 tsp garlic powder

- ❖ 1/2 tsp onion powder

- ❖ 2 Tbsp nutritional yeast

- ❖ 1/8 tsp turmeric

- ❖ 1/2 cup chopped vegetables in season

- ❖ Sea salt

- ❖ Freshly ground black pepper

- ❖ Nonstick cooking spray

## How to Prepare

1. Set the oven to 400 degrees F. Lightly coat a small baking pan and set aside.

2. Crumble the tofu using your fingers into a bowl, then gently mix in the onion and garlic powders, nutritional yeast, turmeric, and Dijon mustard. Add salt and pepper, then mix well.

3. Fold in the chopped vegetables, then pack the mixture into the prepared baking pan.

4. Bake for 15 to 20 minutes, or until firm and pale brown.

5. Remove from the oven and set on a cooling rack for 3 minutes. Flip over on a platter, then serve right away.

# Chia Pudding with Pomegranate Seeds

*Makes 2 servings*

## Ingredients

- ❖ 2 cups coconut milk
- ❖ 1/2 cup chia seeds
- ❖ 1 Tbsp pure maple syrup
- ❖ 1 Tbsp unsweetened shredded coconut
- ❖ 2 Tbsp pomegranate seeds

## How to Prepare

1. Combine the maple syrup and coconut milk in a bowl.

2. Add the chia seeds and shredded coconut, then stir well to combine. Cover the bowl and refrigerate overnight.

3. The next morning, uncover and sprinkle the pomegranate seeds on top. Serve right away.

# Brown Rice Johnnycakes

*Makes 4 servings*

## Ingredients

- ❖ 1/4 cup brown rice flour
- ❖ 1/4 cup whole wheat flour
- ❖ 1/2 cup nut milk
- ❖ 1/2 Tbsp baking powder
- ❖ 1/16 tsp fine sea salt
- ❖ 1/4 tsp ground cinnamon
- ❖ 1 Tbsp pure maple syrup
- ❖ Nonstick cooking spray

## How to Prepare

1. Combine the salt, baking powder, cinnamon, brown rice flour, and whole wheat flour in a mixing bowl.

2. In a separate bowl, combine the maple syrup and nut milk. Gently mix the wet ingredients into the dry ingredients until combined; take care not to over-mix.

3. Set aside for 8 minutes.

4. Coat a pancake griddle with nonstick cooking spray, then place it over the lowest possible flame.

5. Ladle about a quarter cup of the batter onto the griddle and cook for 3 minutes per side, or until firm. Transfer to a platter and serve right away with fresh fruit and/or pure maple syrup.

## *Granola Cereal*
*Makes 1 1/2 lbs*

### Ingredients

- ❖ 1 3/4 cups rolled oats

- ❖ 1 cup raw chopped nuts of any kind (such as almonds, pecans, walnuts and/or cashews)

- ❖ 1/2 cup unsweetened shredded coconut

- ❖ 1/2 cup raw pumpkin and/or sunflower seeds

- ❖ 3/4 tsp ground ginger

- ❖ 1 tsp ground cinnamon

- ❖ 1/4 tsp ground nutmeg

- ❖ 1/4 tsp fine sea salt

- ❖ 3 Tbsp coconut oil

- ❖ 1/4 cup pure maple syrup

- ❖ 1 tsp pure vanilla extract

### How to Prepare

1. Set the oven to 250 degrees F. Cover a large rimmed baking sheet with baking paper and set aside.

2. In a bowl, combine the oats, seeds, nuts, salt, spices, and shredded coconut.

3. Place a pot over low flame and melt the coconut oil and maple syrup together. Let simmer until the coconut oil is liquefied then stir in the vanilla extract.

4. Fold the oil mixture into the bowl of oat mixture. Mix everything well using a rubber spatula.

5. Spread the mixture on the prepared baking sheet as thinly as possible. Place into the oven and bake for 30 to 45 minutes or until crisp.

6. Remove from the oven and set on a cooling rack. Allow to cool completely, then transfer to a large, airtight jar. Store for up to 14 days on a cool, dry shelf. Serve with nut milk.

# Sweet Potato Hash Browns

*Makes 6 servings*

## Ingredients

- ❖ 3 medium sweet potatoes, scrubbed and diced

- ❖ 2 small apples, cored and diced

- ❖ 1 1/4 tsp dried rosemary

- ❖ Sea salt

- ❖ Freshly ground black pepper

- ❖ Nonstick cooking spray

## How to Prepare

1. Set the oven to 400 degrees F. Lightly coat a baking sheet with nonstick cooking spray and set aside.

2. Using a spice grinder or mortar and pestle, grind the rosemary until coarsely ground, then set aside.

3. Spread the diced sweet potatoes and apples on the prepared baking sheet, then season with the ground rosemary, salt, and pepper. Toss to coat.

4. Spread the mixture to create an even layer, then bake for 25 minutes, or until crisp and golden brown. Serve warm.

# Dates and Oats Energy Bars

*Makes 18 pieces*

## Ingredients

- ❖ 2 1/4 cups quick cooking oats
- ❖ 2 cups whole wheat pastry flour
- ❖ 1 1/2 cups unsweetened nut milk
- ❖ 1 1/2 cups unsweetened applesauce
- ❖ 3/4 cup pureed dates
- ❖ 3/4 tsp sea salt
- ❖ 3 tsp baking powder
- ❖ 1 1/2 tsp ground cinnamon
- ❖ 3/4 cup organic peanut butter
- ❖ 1/3 cup pure maple syrup
- ❖ 1 1/2 tsp pure vanilla extract

## How to Prepare

1. Set the oven to 350 degrees F. Line a baking dish with baking paper and set aside.

2. In a large mixing bowl, mix together the oats, baking powder, salt, cinnamon, and flour.

3. In a separate bowl, mix together the nut milk, pureed dates, peanut butter, vanilla extract, applesauce and maple syrup. Fold the wet ingredients into the dry ingredients until just combined.

4. Pour the batter into the prepared baking dish and pack firmly using a rubber spatula. Bake for 20 to 25 minutes. Check for readiness by poking the center with a toothpick; if it comes out clean, it is ready.

5. Set on a cooling rack for at least 25 minutes, then slice into 18 even pieces and serve at once or store in an airtight jar for up to 5 days.

## Savory Scrambled Garbanzo Beans

*Makes 2 servings*

### Ingredients

- ❖ 1 1/4 tsp extra virgin olive oil
- ❖ 1 large shallot, minced
- ❖ 1/2 cup chickpea flour
- ❖ 1 1/2 Tbsp freshly squeezed lemon juice
- ❖ 1 green hot chili, seeded and minced
- ❖ 3/4 cup warm water
- ❖ 1/3 tsp sea salt

### How to Prepare

1. Place the chickpea flour into a saucepan and place over medium low flame. Toast, stirring frequently, until golden and fragrant. Scrape into a bowl and set aside.

2. Heat 1/4 teaspoon of extra virgin olive oil in the same saucepan, then stir in the chili and shallots. Sauté until shallots are tender. Transfer to a saucer.

3. Pour the water and lemon juice into the saucepan and stir in the salt. Set to medium

flame, then stir in the chickpea flour. Whisk well until combined and thickened. Continue to mix into a dough.

4. Fold in the shallots and chili mixture, then scramble and transfer to a plate. Serve right away.

# Cinnamon and Raisin Rice Pudding

*Makes 2 servings*

## Ingredients

- ❖ 2 1/4 cups cooked leftover brown rice

- ❖ 2 1/2 Tbsp pure maple syrup

- ❖ 1/2 cup raisins (or other chopped dried fruit)

- ❖ 3/4 cup nut milk

- ❖ 1 tsp ground cinnamon

- ❖ 1/2 tsp pure almond or vanilla extract

- ❖ Sea salt

- ❖ Optional: 1/4 cup toasted chopped nuts, such as almonds

## How to Prepare

1. Combine the milk and maple syrup in a saucepan over medium flame. Stir in the rice.

2. Add the extract, cinnamon, raisins, and a dash of salt. Stir until rice has fully absorbed the milk. Top with chopped nuts, then serve right away.

## Silken Tofu Omelet

*Makes 4 servings*

### Ingredients

- ❖ 250 oz silken tofu, extra firm
- ❖ 4 Tbsp cornstarch
- ❖ 4 Tbsp chickpea flour
- ❖ 4 Tbsp nutritional yeast
- ❖ 1 1/2 tsp turmeric
- ❖ 1 tsp onion powder
- ❖ 1 tsp garlic powder
- ❖ 1/2 cup nut milk
- ❖ Sea salt
- ❖ Freshly ground black pepper
- ❖ Nonstick cooking spray

### How to Prepare

1. Set the oven to 350 degrees F. Lightly coat a shallow baking dish with nonstick cooking spray and set aside.

2. In a food processor, blend the tofu, cornstarch, chickpea flour, nutritional yeast,

turmeric, onion powder, garlic powder and nut milk until smooth.

3. Season with salt and pepper, then blend again to combine.

4. Pour the mixture into the prepared baking dish, then bake for 30 minutes, or until firm. Set on a cooling rack for about 8 minutes, then slice and serve. Excess batter can be stored in an airtight container and refrigerated for up to 4 days.

# Chapter 3 - Soups

## Smooth Cauliflower and Mushroom Soup
*Makes 6 servings*

### Ingredients

- ❖ 3 Tbsp olive oil
- ❖ 2 cups chopped cauliflower
- ❖ 6 Tbsp red wine vinegar
- ❖ 3 large onions, chopped
- ❖ 2 1/4 lb sliced cremini mushrooms
- ❖ 4 1/2 cups vegetable stock
- ❖ 3 Tbsp minced fresh dill
- ❖ 2 1/4 Tbsp paprika
- ❖ Sea salt
- ❖ Freshly ground black pepper

### How to Prepare

1. Combine the olive oil, cauliflower, 3 tablespoons of red wine vinegar, and a pinch of

salt in a food processor. Blend until pureed. Set aside.

2. Place a large saucepan over medium flame and add 1 tablespoon of water. Let simmer, then add the mushrooms and onion and sauté until tender, adding a bit of water constantly to prevent drying out.

3. Stir the vegetable stock, paprika, pureed cauliflower, and dill into the saucepan. Simmer over medium flame for about 15 minutes.

4. Stir in the remaining red wine vinegar and season to taste with salt and pepper. Transfer to a bowl and serve right away.

# Savory Sweet Potato Soup
*Makes 3 servings*

## Ingredients

- ❖ 1/2 Tbsp olive oil
- ❖ 2 medium sweet potatoes, peeled and diced
- ❖ 1 large leek, white and light green parts, rinsed thoroughly and diced
- ❖ 1 medium red bell pepper, seeded and diced
- ❖ 2 cups vegetable stock
- ❖ Zest of 1/2 orange
- ❖ 1/2 tsp dried rosemary
- ❖ 1/8 tsp nutmeg
- ❖ Sea salt
- ❖ Freshly ground black pepper

## How to Prepare

1. Place a saucepan over medium flame and heat the olive oil. Sauté the red bell pepper and leeks until tender.

2. Stir in the sweet potatoes, orange zest, nutmeg, rosemary, and vegetable stock.

Increase to high flame and let boil, then reduce to medium flame and simmer for 8 minutes, or until sweet potatoes are tender.

3. Season to taste with salt and pepper, then turn off the heat and let stand for 5 minutes.

4. Transfer the solids into a food processor or blender using a slotted spoon, then blend until smooth. Pour back into the saucepan and stir well to combine. Reheat if necessary, then serve right away.

## Yam and Kale Soup
*Makes 4 servings*

### Ingredients

- ❖ 2 small red onions, sliced thinly
- ❖ 1/2 cup water
- ❖ 4 cups peeled and diced yams
- ❖ 5 cups vegetable stock
- ❖ 10 cups roughly chopped kale
- ❖ 2 tsp garlic powder
- ❖ 2 Tbsp yellow miso paste
- ❖ 4 tsp chili powder
- ❖ 2 tsp mild curry powder
- ❖ 2 tsp cumin
- ❖ 1/2 tsp red pepper flakes
- ❖ 1/2 tsp cinnamon

### How to Prepare

1. Place a large stock pot over medium high flame and add the water. Let simmer, then add the onion and simmer until translucent.

2. Stir in the vegetable stock and yams, then let boil. Once boiling, reduce to medium flame and simmer until yams are fork tender.

3. Add the kale, garlic powder, miso paste, chili, curry, cumin, red pepper flakes, and cinnamon. Stir and let simmer until the kale is wilted.

4. Turn off the heat and let sit for 5 minutes, then serve piping hot.

# Chilled Sweet Red Soup

*Makes 4 servings*

## Ingredients

- ❖ 3/4 cups apple and/or cranberry juice
- ❖ 4 Tbsp pure maple syrup
- ❖ 4 oz sliced rhubarb
- ❖ 8 oz sliced strawberries
- ❖ 1 cinnamon stick
- ❖ 2 Tbsp raisins
- ❖ 1 Tbsp cornstarch or arrowroot powder
- ❖ 2 Tbsp water

## How to Prepare

1. Combine the rhubarb, strawberries, maple syrup, and cinnamon stick in a saucepan over medium high flame and let boil. Stir in the raisins.

2. Once boiling, reduce to low flame and let simmer for about 12 minutes.

3. Combine the cornstarch and water in a small bowl, then stir into the saucepan. Stir the mixture until thickened.

4. Turn off the heat and allow to cool slightly. Transfer to a bowl, cover, and refrigerate for at least 2 hours or until chilled.

# Golden Split Pea Soup
*Makes 4 servings*

## Ingredients

- ❖ 2 cups dried yellow split peas, rinsed and drained thoroughly

- ❖ 4 cups water

- ❖ 1/2 tsp ground ginger

- ❖ 2 tsp garam masala

- ❖ 1 tsp cumin

- ❖ 1 tsp turmeric

- ❖ 1/4 tsp cayenne powder

- ❖ Sea salt

## How to Prepare

1. Boil the water in a pot, then stir in the split peas.

2. Add the garam masala, turmeric, ginger, cumin, and cayenne. Stir, then reduce to low flame. Cover and let simmer for half an hour, or until the split peas are tender.

3. Season to taste with salt, then serve with steamed greens.

# Hot Mung Bean Soup
*Makes 4 servings*

## Ingredients

- ❖ 2 tsp canola oil
- ❖ 1 small red onion, sliced thinly
- ❖ 3/4 tsp minced garlic
- ❖ 1 large tomato, chopped
- ❖ 2 1/2 cups vegetable stock
- ❖ 1/2 cup coconut milk
- ❖ Juice of 1/2 lemon
- ❖ 1/2 cup dried mung beans, rinsed thoroughly
- ❖ 1/2 tsp cumin
- ❖ 1/2 tsp garam masala
- ❖ 1/4 tsp turmeric
- ❖ 1/4 tsp curry powder
- ❖ 1/4 cup minced fresh cilantro
- ❖ 1 Tbsp minced fresh ginger
- ❖ 1/2 small serrano pepper, sliced thinly
- ❖ Sea salt

## How to Prepare

1. Mix together the curry powder, turmeric, garam masala, and cumin in a small bowl. Set aside.

2. Combine the vegetable stock and mung beans in a pot, then place over medium flame and let simmer for about 30 minutes, or until the beans are tender. Turn off the heat and set aside.

3. Place another pot over medium high flame and heat the canola oil. Stir in the onion and sauté for 8 minutes or until golden brown. Set to medium low flame and stir in the ginger, tomatoes, and garlic until fragrant.

4. Add the spice mixture into the pot and stir until fragrant, then stir in the beans and stock mixture. Let simmer, then stir in the coconut milk.

5. Reduce to low flame and continue to simmer for about 8 minutes. Add the cilantro and stir in the lemon juice. Season to taste with salt, then serve right away.

# Baked Sweet Potato Curry Soup

*Makes 4 servings*

## Ingredients

- ❖ 1 yellow onion, chopped
- ❖ 6 garlic cloves, minced
- ❖ 2 medium sweet potatoes
- ❖ 2 cups vegetable stock
- ❖ 1/2 tsp garam masala
- ❖ 1 tsp mild curry powder
- ❖ 1 cup nut milk
- ❖ 1/2 cup cooked black or wild rice

## How to Prepare

1. Set the oven to 425 degrees F.

2. Poke the sweet potatoes with a fork, then bake for 45 minutes.

3. Set the baked sweet potatoes on a cooling rack and allow to cool completely, then remove the skins.

4. Transfer the peeled sweet potatoes into a blender or food processor, then puree and set aside.

44

5. Pour the vegetable stock into large saucepan then place over medium high flame Stir in the onion and garlic, 1/2 teaspoon of garam masala, and 1 teaspoon of the curry. Let boil, then reduce to low flame. Place the lid on and let simmer for 5 minutes.

6. Turn off the heat and let the mixture cool slightly. Pour into a blender and add the pureed sweet potato. Pour in the milk and blend until smooth.

7. Pour the mixture back into the saucepan and place over medium flame. Heat through, then stir in the remaining ingredients, except the rice.

8. Divide the soup into four servings, then spoon the cooked rice on top. Serve right away.

# Creamy Carrot and Squash Soup

*Makes 5 servings*

## Ingredients

- ❖ 1/2 Tbsp olive oil
- ❖ 1 small onion, chopped
- ❖ 1 quart vegetable stock
- ❖ 2 medium carrots, chopped
- ❖ 1 1/2 lb butternut squash, peeled and chopped into chunks
- ❖ 1/2 Tbsp minced fresh ginger
- ❖ 1 Tbsp grated orange zest
- ❖ 3 Tbsp chopped fresh flat-leaf parsley
- ❖ Ground nutmeg
- ❖ Sea salt
- ❖ Freshly ground white pepper

## How to Prepare

1. Place a saucepan over medium flame and heat the olive oil. Add the onion, carrot, ginger, and squash and sauté until golden brown and tender.

2. Pour the vegetable stock into the pot, then add the orange zest. Increase to medium high flame and let boil, then reduce to low flame and cook for 25 to 30 minutes, uncovered, or until the vegetables are very tender.

3. Stir in the parsley and season with a dash each of salt, pepper, and nutmeg.

4. Turn off the heat and let cool slightly, then transfer the solids into a food processor or blender and puree, or use an immersion blender. Reheat if necessary, then serve right away.

# Squash and Tomato Soup
*Makes 3 servings*

## Ingredients

- ❖ 5 cups peeled plum tomatoes, juices reserved
- ❖ 1 cup cooked shredded spaghetti squash
- ❖ 5 baby carrots, minced
- ❖ 1 garlic clove, minced
- ❖ 1 cup vegetable stock
- ❖ 1/2 Tbsp onion powder
- ❖ 1 tsp Italian seasoning
- ❖ 1/2 Tbsp white vinegar
- ❖ 1/2 bay leaf
- ❖ 1/2 tsp mild curry powder
- ❖ 1 tsp agave nectar
- ❖ Garlic powder
- ❖ Sea salt
- ❖ Freshly ground white pepper

## How to Prepare

1. Place the plum tomatoes and their juices into a stock pot, then mash well with a fork.

2. Stir in the carrot, vinegar, garlic, curry powder, onion powder, Italian seasoning, red pepper flakes, vinegar, bay leaf and a dash each of salt, and white pepper.

3. Cover the pot and place over high flame. Bring to a boil, then reduce to a simmer. Let simmer over low flame for 15 to 20 minutes.

4. Stir in the agave nectar and simmer for 3 minutes. Discard the bay leaf and season to taste, if necessary.

5. Ladle the soup into three bowls, then top with the spaghetti squash and serve right away.

## *Hearty Vegetable Soup*

*Makes 4 servings*

### Ingredients

- ❖ 1/2 Tbsp canola oil

- ❖ 3 cups vegetable stock or cold water

- ❖ 2 1/2 cups pure tomato juice

- ❖ 1 small onion, diced

- ❖ 1 garlic clove, minced

- ❖ 1/4 cup seeded and chopped green bell pepper

- ❖ 1 celery stalk, diced

- ❖ 3 dried shiitake mushrooms

- ❖ 1 cup chopped cauliflower florets

- ❖ 1 cup chopped broccoli florets

- ❖ 1/4 cup barley

- ❖ 1/4 cup rolled whole oats

- ❖ 3/4 cup dried black-eyed peas

- ❖ 1/2 lb button mushrooms, sliced

- ❖ 1 small yellow squash, diced

- ❖ 1 small zucchini, diced

- ❖ 1 Tbsp fresh thyme

- ❖ 1 bay leaf

- ❖ 1/4 cup chopped fresh flat-leaf parsley

- ❖ 1/2 tsp sea salt


**How to Prepare:**

1. Put the black-eyed peas into a pot and add just enough water to cover. Place over medium high flame and boil for 3 to 5 minutes. Turn off the heat and stir in the barley. Let stand for half an hour.

2. In the meantime, Pour 1/2 cup warm water into a small saucepan and add the dried shiitake mushrooms. Place over medium high flame and boil. Once boiling, turn off the heat and let stand for 20 minutes.

3. Remove the shiitake mushrooms from the pot, slice off the stems, then chop the caps and set aside.

4. Place a wok over medium flame and heat the canola oil. Stir in the onion, carrots, celery, cauliflower, broccoli, bell pepper, and garlic. Sprinkle in the thyme and salt, then stir-fry for about 5 minutes or until tender.

5. Pour the vegetable stock or cold water into the pot, then stir in the barley and beans. Stir in the tomato juice and bay leaf, then increase heat to a boil.

6. Stir in the oats, chopped shiitake mushrooms, button mushrooms, zucchini, and squash. Reduce to a simmer.

7. Let simmer for 7 minutes, or until soup liquids become creamy. Remove the bay leaf, add the parsley, and serve right away.

# Bonus Recipe: Homemade Vegetable Stock

*Makes 3 quarts*

## Ingredients

- ❖ 2 medium onions, quartered
- ❖ 5 garlic cloves, peeled and crushed
- ❖ 1 large tomato, quartered
- ❖ 2 medium potatoes, peeled and chopped
- ❖ 3 large carrots, chopped
- ❖ 5 celery stalks, chopped
- ❖ 2 medium leeks, rinsed thoroughly and chopped
- ❖ 1 1/2 pints chopped mushrooms
- ❖ 1 bunch fresh flat-leaf parsley
- ❖ 5 bay leaves
- ❖ 6 whole sprigs fresh thyme
- ❖ 4 1/4 quarts cold filtered water
- ❖ 1 1/2 tsp black peppercorns
- ❖ Sea salt

## How to Prepare

1. Combine all of the ingredients except the peppercorns and salt in a 3 quart stock pot. Place over high flame and let boil.

2. Once boiling ,reduce to low flame, then simmer for 1 hour, uncovered.

3. Stir in the peppercorns and simmer for an additional 20 minutes.

4. Remove the solids using a strainer, then season the stock with salt. Set aside to cool, then divide into desired amounts in airtight containers and freeze for up to 3 months.

# Chapter 4 - Salads

## Simple Caesar Salad
*Makes 3 servings*

### Ingredients

- ❖ 1 romaine lettuce heart, rinsed thoroughly, trimmed, and chopped
- ❖ 2 Roma tomatoes, sliced into rounds
- ❖ 1 small zucchini, sliced into thin rounds
- ❖ 2 garlic cloves, finely minced

### *Dressing*

- ❖ 2 1/2 Tbsp extra virgin olive oil
- ❖ 1 garlic clove, minced
- ❖ 1/2 Tbsp freshly squeezed lemon juice
- ❖ Fine sea salt
- ❖ Freshly ground black pepper
- ❖ Optional: 1 Tbsp freshly grated Parmesan cheese

*Optional: Croutons*

- ❖ 1 Tbsp and 1/2 tsp extra virgin olive oil

- ❖ 3/4 tsp dried Italian seasoning

- ❖ 1/4 tsp garlic powder

- ❖ Fine sea salt

- ❖ 2 slices whole wheat bread, cubed

**How to Prepare**

1. If you want to make croutons, set the oven to 350 degrees F. Combine the olive oil, Italian seasoning, garlic powder, and a dash of sea salt in a bowl, then mix in the cubed bread.

2. Bake for 15 minutes, or until golden brown.

3. Combine all the ingredients for the dressing with a pinch of salt and black pepper. Whisk vigorously.

4. Prepare the salad by laying the romaine lettuce on a platter, then top with the sliced vegetables, minced garlic, and the croutons, if desired.

5. Serve with the salad dressing on the side. To control consumption of dressing, dip the salad fork into the dressing before picking up the salad instead of drizzling the dressing all over the salad.

# Green Papaya Salad

*Makes 4 servings*

## Ingredients

- ❖ 6 cups shredded green papaya
- ❖ 1/2 lb raw green beans, sliced diagonally
- ❖ 20 ripe cherry tomatoes, halved
- ❖ 2 cups chopped cilantro
- ❖ 1 tsp red pepper flakes
- ❖ 6 Tbsp freshly squeezed lime juice
- ❖ 8 tsp grated palm sugar
- ❖ 4 garlic cloves, minced
- ❖ 1 tsp sea salt
- ❖ 2/3 cup ground roasted cashews or peanuts
- ❖ Freshly ground black pepper

## How to Prepare

1. Toss together the green papaya, cherry tomatoes, green beans, red pepper flakes and cilantro in a large bowl. Set aside.

2. In a small bowl, mix together the lime juice palm sugar, garlic, salt, and a dash of black pepper.

3. Drizzle the dressing all over the salad and toss to coat. Sprinkle the ground roasted cashew or peanuts on top, then serve right away.

# Spinach and Bell Pepper Salad

*Makes 2 servings*

## Ingredients

- ❖ 4 cups stemmed and sliced  fresh spinach
- ❖ 1 small red bell pepper, seeded and diced
- ❖ 2 Tbsp thinly sliced green onion
- ❖ Optional: 2 Tbsp toasted sunflower seeds

## *Dressing:*

- ❖ Freshly ground black pepper
- ❖ 2 Tbsp balsamic vinegar
- ❖ 1 Tbsp Dijon mustard
- ❖ 2 Tbsp minced shallot

## How to Prepare

1. To make the dressing, whisk together the vinegar and mustard. Add the shallot and mix well. Season to taste with black pepper.

2. Toss together the spinach, bell pepper, and green onion in a salad bowl. Divide into two servings.

3. Sprinkle the sliced green onion on top of the salad.

4. Serve with the salad dressing on the side. To control consumption of dressing, dip the salad fork into the dressing before picking up the salad instead of drizzling the dressing all over the salad.

# Ginger Cucumber Salad

*Makes 4 to 6 servings*

## Ingredients

* ❖ 1 lb cucumbers, peeled, halved and seeded

* ❖ 6 Tbsp rice vinegar

* ❖ 4 tsp freshly grated ginger

* ❖ 2 Tbsp maple syrup

* ❖ 2 tsp sea salt

* ❖ 4 scallions, green pars, sliced thinly

* ❖ 2 Tbsp toasted sesame seeds

## How to Prepare

1. Combine the rice vinegar, ginger, maple syrup, and salt into a small glass jar. Cover and shake to combine. Refrigerate for 20 minutes.

2. Slice the cucumber halves thinly, then place in a bowl.

3. Shake the dressing again, then drizzle on top of the cucumbers. Sprinkle the sliced scallions and toasted sesame seeds on top, then serve right away.

# Stir-fried Reds and Kale Salad with Peanut Sauce

*Makes 2 servings*

## Ingredients

- ❖ 8 cups stemmed and chopped kale
- ❖ 1 small red onion, sliced thinly
- ❖ 1 small red bell pepper, seeded and diced
- ❖ Optional: 1/2 tsp crushed red pepper flakes
- ❖ Olive oil

## *Sauce*

- ❖ 2 Tbsp creamy organic peanut butter
- ❖ 1 Tbsp brown rice or pure maple syrup
- ❖ 1 Tbsp tamari
- ❖ 1 Tbsp rice vinegar
- ❖ 1/3 tsp ground ginger
- ❖ Optional: cayenne pepper

## How to Prepare

1. Whisk together all of the ingredients for the sauce in a bowl. Season with a dash of cayenne pepper, if desired. Set aside.

2. Place a large nonstick skillet over medium flame and heat just enough olive oil to coat the bottom.

3. Sauté the red onion and bell pepper until onion is translucent and bell pepper is tender.

4. Gradually add the kale and stir until wilted, gradually drizzling in the peanut sauce. Season with the crushed red pepper flakes, if desired.

5. Transfer the salad to a plate and serve right away.

# Fennel and Orange Salad

*Makes 2 servings*

## Ingredients

- ❖ 1/2 lb fennel

- ❖ 1 small navel orange

- ❖ 1/2 Tbsp freshly squeezed lemon juice

- ❖ 1 tsp olive oil

- ❖ 1/4 tsp freshly grated lemon zest

- ❖ 1/4 cup sliced pitted kalamata olives

- ❖ 1/4 tsp sea salt

- ❖ 1/4 tsp hot paprika

- ❖ 1/8 tsp freshly ground black pepper

## How to Prepare

1. Use a vegetable peeler, sharp knife, or mandolin to peel the fennel into extra thin shreds. Place into a bowl.

2. Gently mix the lemon juice and zest with the fennel, then set aside.

3. Peel the orange and slice into extra thin rounds using a sharp knife.

4. Transfer the fennel onto a platter, spreading out into an even layer.

5. Place the sliced oranges on top, then drizzle the olive oil and season with paprika, salt, and pepper. Serve right away.

## Artichoke and Garbanzo Bean Salad with Tomato Dressing

*Makes 6 servings*

### Ingredients

- ❖ 2 small red onions, diced

- ❖ 3/4 cup sun-dried tomatoes, dry not soaked

- ❖ 6 cups fresh greens, such as arugula

- ❖ 1 1/2 cups chopped fresh basil leaves

- ❖ 45 oz canned garbanzo beans, drained and rinsed thoroughly

- ❖ 25 oz canned artichoke hearts in brine, chopped

- ❖ 4 1/2 Tbsp red wine vinegar

- ❖ Optional: 3 Tbsp toasted chopped nuts or seeds, such as pine nuts or sunflower seeds

- ❖ Sea salt

- ❖ Freshly ground black pepper

### How to Prepare

1. Place the sun-dried tomatoes into a saucepan and add just enough water to cover them.

66

2. Place over medium flame and let simmer for about 10 to 12 minutes or until very tender. Remove from heat and set aside to cool slightly.

3. Transfer the tomatoes into a blender, then blend until smooth. Transfer to a bowl.

4. Stir the red wine vinegar into the tomato puree, then add the garbanzo beans, red onion, basil, and artichoke hearts. Toss well to coat, seasoning with salt and pepper.

5. Lay the arugula on a platter, then heap the salad on top. Serve right away.

## Quinoa Salad with Dates and Pistachios

*Makes 2 servings*

### Ingredients

- ❖ 1/2 cup white quinoa, rinsed and drained thoroughly

- ❖ 1 1/2 cups tender baby greens, such as spinach

- ❖ 1/2 small white onion, sliced into wedges

- ❖ 1/2 cup chopped pitted medjool dates

- ❖ 1/2 cup cooked garbanzo beans

- ❖ 3/4 cup water

- ❖ 1/4 tsp sea salt

- ❖ 1/2 tsp fennel seeds

- ❖ 1/2 tsp cumin seeds

- ❖ 1/4 cup chopped fresh flat-leaf parsley

- ❖ 2 1/2 Tbsp chopped toasted pistachio nuts

*Dressing:*

- ❖ 1 1/2 Tbsp freshly squeezed lemon juice

- ❖ 1 Tbsp extra virgin olive oil

- ❖  1/4 tsp sea salt

- ❖  1/4 tsp ground coriander

- ❖  Freshly ground black pepper

## How to Prepare

1. Place the quinoa into a stock pot and place over medium flame. Stir frequently for 3 minutes until toasted and dry.

2. Stir in the fennel seeds and cumin, then toast for 1 minute.

3. Stir in the water and salt, then bring to a boil. Stir, then cover and set to low flame. Cook for 10 to 12 minutes, or until the quinoa has fully absorbed the liquid and is fluffy.

4. Fluff up the quinoa and cover the pot. Set aside.

5. Meanwhile, toss together the onion, dates, greens, garbanzo beans, pistachios, and parsley in a bowl. Set aside.

6. Combine all the ingredients for the dressing in a bowl. Whisk well and drizzle over the greens mixture. Toss to coat.

7. Add the quinoa and toss well to coat, then serve right away.

# Healthy Potato Salad

*Makes 3 servings*

## Ingredients

- ❖ 1 lb organic red skin potatoes or sweet potatoes, scrubbed and cubed

- ❖ 2 green onions, thinly sliced

- ❖ 1/4 cup toasted pine nuts

- ❖ 2 Tbsp minced fresh dill

- ❖ 1/4 cup pitted kalamata olives

- ❖ Sea salt

- ❖ Freshly ground black pepper

## *Dressing:*

- ❖ 2 Tbsp olive oil

- ❖ 1/2 cup chopped cauliflower

- ❖ 1 Tbsp red wine vinegar

- ❖ 1/4 tsp sea salt

## How to Prepare

1. Fill a medium pot with cold water and add some salt. Place the potatoes into the pot, then

cover and place over medium high flame. Boil for about 8 minutes, or until potatoes are tender.

2. To make the dressing, place the cauliflower and olive oil inside a food processor and process until pureed. Add the vinegar and sea salt, then blend until thoroughly combined.

3. Drain the boiled potatoes, then place under cold running water. Let cool, then cube and place into a bowl.

4. Add the dressing to the potatoes, then the dill, olives, and pine nuts. Season lightly with salt and pepper, then toss well to coat.

5. Cover the bowl and refrigerate for at least 1 hour. Serve chilled.

# Crunchy Avocado and Mango Salad

*Makes 4 servings*

## Ingredients

- ❖ 2 ripe avocados
- ❖ 2 ripe mangoes, peeled and diced
- ❖ 2 cups chopped fresh cilantro
- ❖ 2 Tbsp chopped fresh mint
- ❖ 2 red onions, peeled and diced
- ❖ 4 Tbsp freshly squeezed lime juice
- ❖ 1 1/2 Tbsp agave nectar
- ❖ 1/2 cup chopped roasted cashews
- ❖ 1/2 tsp sea salt
- ❖ 1/4 tsp freshly ground white pepper

## How to Prepare

1. In a large bowl, combine the lime juice, salt, white pepper, and agave nectar.

2. Halve the avocados, then remove the core and scoop out the flesh. Slice into cubes and add into the bowl. Toss gently to coat.

3. Add the red onion, mint, cilantro, mango, and cashews. Toss well to combine, then divide into four servings and serve right away.

# Chapter 5 - Main Dishes

## *Aubergine Ragout*

*Makes 6 servings*

### Ingredients

- ❖ 1 Tbsp olive oil

- ❖ 2 small yellow onions, diced

- ❖ 2 medium tomatoes, diced

- ❖ 12 cups cubed eggplants

- ❖ 1 1/2 cups pitted kalamata olives

- ❖ 1 1/2 cups fresh basil leaves

- ❖ 10 oz canned garbanzo beans, drained and rinsed thoroughly

- ❖ 1 1/2 Tbsp freshly squeezed lemon juice

- ❖ 1 large garlic clove

- ❖ 1 tsp sea salt

### How to Prepare

1. First make the basil paste by combining the garbanzo beans, garlic, lemon juice, and salt in the food processor. Blend until smooth, adding

just a bit of water if needed to maintain creaminess. Set aside.

2. Place a nonstick skillet over medium flame and heat the olive oil. Sauté the onion and cubed eggplant for about 10 minutes, adding a bit of water to prevent burning.

3. Stir in the kalamata olives and tomatoes, then sauté for 5 minutes.

4. Stir in the basil paste and let simmer as you stir constantly. Transfer to a platter and serve right away.

# Veggie Brown Rice Risotto

*Makes 6 servings*

## Ingredients

- ❖ 2 1/2 Tbsp olive oil

- ❖ 2 small garlic cloves, minced

- ❖ 3/4 cup diced onion

- ❖ 1 1/2 cups whole grain brown rice, quick-cooking

- ❖ 5 1/2 cups vegetable stock

- ❖ 2 cups diced mixed vegetables, preferably roasted (such as mushrooms, broccoli, asparagus, Brussels sprouts, bell pepper)

- ❖ Fine sea salt

- ❖ Freshly ground black pepper

- ❖ Optional: 1/3 dry white wine

- ❖ Optional: 2/3 cup grated Parmigiano-Reggiano cheese

## How to Prepare

1. Simmer the vegetable stock in a pot over medium low flame.

2. Place a heavy-bottomed saucepan over medium flame and heat the olive oil. Saute the onion until tender, then stir in the garlic and saute until fragrant.

3. Stir in the brown rice and saute for about 4 minutes, mixing well with the oil, garlic and onion. Pour in the wine, if using, and continue to stir until completely evaporated.

4. Set heat to medium low, then pour about a cup of the simmering vegetable stock into the saucepan. Stir frequently as it gently simmers until the rice has almost absorbed the stick. Continue to gradually add the stock as you stir until the risotto is moist and fluffy.

5. Fold in the roasted vegetables, then season to taste with salt and pepper. If desired, top with cheese.

# Pad Thai

*Makes 4 servings*

## Ingredients

- ❖ 1/2 lb thick rice noodles
- ❖ 6 oz bean sprouts
- ❖ 2 Tbsp creamy peanut butter
- ❖ 4 Tbsp tamari
- ❖ 2 Tbsp sweet red chili Asian sauce
- ❖ 1/2 tsp ground ginger
- ❖ 1/2 tsp garlic powder
- ❖ 1/2 tsp hot sauce
- ❖ 1 lime, sliced into wedges

## How to Prepare

1. Cook the rice noodles based on manufacturer's instructions. Drain and set aside.

2. In a large bowl, combine about 4 tablespoons of warm water with the peanut butter, tamari, chili sauce, ginger, hot sauce, and garlic powder. Mix well.

3. Add the cooked rice noodles into the bowl of sauce and toss carefully with a pair of tongs to coat.

4. Transfer the Pad Thai to a platter and add the bean sprouts on top. Serve right away with the lime wedges.

# Vegan Chili

*Makes 6 servings*

## Ingredients

- ❖ 3 Tbsp olive oil

- ❖ 3 garlic cloves, minced

- ❖ 2 bell peppers, seeded and diced

- ❖ 42 oz jarred diced tomatoes, juices reserved

- ❖ 1 1/4 cups corn kernels (fresh or frozen)

- ❖ 1 1/4 cups diced onion

- ❖ 25 oz canned kidney beans, drained and rinsed thoroughly

- ❖ 1 1/2 tsp ground cumin

- ❖ 1/6 tsp cayenne pepper

- ❖ 3 tsp chili powder

- ❖ 1 1/2 tsp sea salt

- ❖ 3 bay leaves

- ❖ 1 avocado

## How to Prepare

1. Place a heavy-bottomed stock pot over medium flame and heat the olive oil. Stir in

the bell pepper and onion and sauté until onion is translucent and bell pepper is tender.

2.  Add the garlic and corn, then sauté until fragrant.

3.  Stir in the beans, tomatoes and their juices, spices, salt, and bay leaves. Increase to high flame and let boil, then reduce to low flame and simmer.

4.  Simmer for 35 to 40 minutes, uncovered, or until thickened. Discard the bay leaves. Ladle into bowls.

5.  Slice the avocado in half, then remove the core. Scoop out the flesh and slice into cubes. Top the chili with avocado cubes, then serve right away.

# Teriyaki Garbanzo Beans

*Makes 4 servings*

## Ingredients

❖ 30 oz canned garbanzo beans, drained and rinsed thoroughly

❖ 4 cups cooked greens or brown rice

❖ 1/2 cup vegan-approved teriyaki sauce

❖ 2 Tbsp hot sauce

❖ 1/2 cup pineapple chunks

❖ Optional: 1/2 cup cubed fresh mango

## How to Prepare

1. In a saucepan, mix together the garbanzo beans, teriyaki sauce, and hot sauce. Set aside for 10 minutes to let the flavors meld.

2. Place the saucepan over medium flame and let simmer, stirring frequently, for about 10 minutes or until the sauce is thickened.

3. Divide the rice into four servings, then top with the teriyaki garbanzo beans. Spoon the pineapple chunks and mango chunks, if using, on top. Serve right away.

# Zesty Navy Beans and Quinoa Bowls

*Makes 2 servings*

## Ingredients

- ❖ 3/4 cup quinoa, rinsed thoroughly
- ❖ 1 Tbsp dried basil
- ❖ 1 1/2 cups vegetable stock
- ❖ 2 garlic cloves, minced
- ❖ 7.5 oz canned navy beans, drained and rinsed thoroughly
- ❖ Juice of 1/2 lemon
- ❖ 1/2 cup chopped pitted kalamata olives
- ❖ Sea salt
- ❖ Freshly ground black pepper

## How to Prepare

1. Mix together the stock and quinoa in a pot, then place over medium high flame and bring to a boil.

2. Once boiling, cover tightly and set to medium flame. Cook for 12 to 15 minutes, or until quinoa is fluffy and has completely absorbed the stock.

83

3. In the meantime, place a non-stick skillet over medium flame and gently simmer 1 tablespoon of water. Add the onion and sauté for 8 minutes, or until very tender.

4. Stir the olives, basil, and garlic in with the onions, then sauté for 4 minutes.

5. Spoon the cooked quinoa into the skillet and add the lemon juice. Season to taste with salt and pepper, then mix well and sauté for about 3 minutes.

**6.** Divide the mixture between two bowls and serve right away.

# Fancy Baked Pineapple Rice with Veggies

*Makes 6 servings*

## Ingredients

- ❖ 1 1/2 Tbsp canola oil
- ❖ 1 1/2 Tbsp toasted sesame oil
- ❖ 1/3 cup minced red onion
- ❖ 1 large pineapple, halved lengthwise
- ❖ 3 Tbsp tamari
- ❖ 3 Tbsp sweet chili sauce
- ❖ 12 oz extra firm tofu
- ❖ 4 1/2 cups hot cooked white rice
- ❖ 3/4 cup cooked peas and carrots
- ❖ 1/3 cup cooked chopped baby corn
- ❖ Sea salt
- ❖ Freshly ground black pepper
- ❖ Nonstick cooking spray

## How to Prepare

1. Set the oven to 325 degrees F.

2. Rinse the tofu under gentle cold running water, then place on a deep dish. Place a smaller dish on top and then place a heavy can on top to drain. Set aside for up to 1 hour, then drain the water.

3. Slice the tofu into cubes, then set aside.

4. Scoop the pineapple flesh out of the halves using a tablespoon. Make sure to have a thin layer of flesh left in the shell. Chop the flesh and set aside.

5. Cut out large sheets of aluminum foil that can almost wrap the pineapple shells, but can leave a small opening in the center. Lightly coat the inner sides of the fol with nonstick cooking spray and set aside.

6. Place a wok over medium flame and heat the canola oil. Stir in the tofu and cook until golden brown.

7. Stir in the red onion and saute until tender, then stir in the chili sauce, tamari, and sesame oil. Saute until simmering, then stir in the rice, peas, carrots, and corn. Season with salt and pepper, then saute for 2 minutes.

8. Stir in the chopped pineapple, then turn off the heat and let cool slightly.

9. Heap the rice mixture into the pineapple shells, then wrap in the prepared sheets of aluminum foil, leaving a small opening in the center.

10. Place the wrapped up shells on a baking sheet and bake for half an hour.

11. Carefully remove from the oven, unwrap, and serve right away.

## Savory Stir-fried Chinese Mustard Cabbage and Tofu

*Makes 6 servings*

### Ingredients

- ❖ 1 1/2 lb firm tofu, sliced into 6 even servings
- ❖ 5 garlic cloves
- ❖ 3 tsp toasted sesame oil
- ❖ 1/3 cup tamari
- ❖ 3 tsp minced fresh ginger
- ❖ 1 1/2 Tbsp sesame seeds
- ❖ 1 1/2 Tbsp pure maple syrup
- ❖ 1 1/4 cups pineapple juice or apple juice
- ❖ 1 1/2 Tbsp cider vinegar or rice vinegar
- ❖ 2 Tbsp miso
- ❖ 1 1/2 tsp crushed red chili flakes

*For the Chinese Mustard Cabbage*

- ❖ 1/2 tsp canola oil
- ❖ 1/2 tsp sesame oil
- ❖ 1/2 tsp minced garlic

88

- ❖  1/2 tsp minced fresh ginger

- ❖  1 small head of bok choy, rinsed thoroughly and sliced

- ❖  1/2 Tbsp tamari

- ❖  4 scallions, sliced

## How to Prepare

1. In a food processor, combine the ginger, garlic, tamari, sesame oil, vinegar, maple syrup, miso, pineapple or apple juice, red chili flakes, and sesame seeds that are not for the Chinese mustard cabbage. Blend until smooth.

2. Pour the marinade into a shallow bowl and add the sliced tofu. Turn to coat in the mixture, then refrigerate from 2 to 8 hours to marinate.

3. Set the oven to 185 degrees F.

4. Place a large wok over high flame and heat the canola oil. Using a slotted spoon, drain the tofu from the marinade and transfer to the wok. Sear the tofu for 2 minutes per side or until golden brown; turn only once.

5. Place the tofu on an ovenproof platter and place in the preheated oven to keep warm.

6. Heat the sesame oil in the same wok, then reduce to medium flame. Stir in the cabbage, ginger, and garlic. Stir-fry for 3 minutes, then stir in the scallions and tamari. Stir fry until heated through, then turn off the heat.

7. Transfer the stir-fried vegetables onto a platter, then place the warmed tofu on top. Drizzle the remaining marinade all over everything, then serve right away.

# Stir-fried Bamboo Shoots and Mushrooms

*Makes 2 servings*

## Ingredients

- ❖ 1 lb bamboo shoots, rinsed and drained
- ❖ 1/2 Tbsp peanut oil
- ❖ 1 garlic clove, minced
- ❖ 1/4 lb fresh shiitake mushrooms, stems removed, sliced thinly
- ❖ 1/2 tsp agave nectar
- ❖ 2 Tbsp vegetable stock
- ❖ Sea salt
- ❖ Freshly ground black pepper

## How to Prepare

1. Place a wok over medium high flame and heat the oil. Stir in the garlic and mushrooms and saute for 2 minutes.

2. Stir in the bamboo shoots, vegetable stock, and agave nectar. Stir fry for 2 minutes, then season to taste with salt and pepper.

3. Transfer to a serving dish and serve right away.

## Spiced Quinoa-Stuffed Bell Peppers

*Makes 9 servings*

### Ingredients

- ❖ 3 large red bell peppers, halved and seeded
- ❖ 3 large green bell peppers, halved and seeded
- ❖ 3 cups vegetable stock
- ❖ 1 1/2 cups quinoa, rinsed and drained thoroughly
- ❖ 2/3 tsp cayenne pepper
- ❖ Sea salt
- ❖ Olive oil

*Stuffing:*

- ❖ 4 1/4 Tbsp olive oil
- ❖ 1/4 cup shelled raw pumpkin seeds
- ❖ 3 celery stalks, minced
- ❖ 1 large carrot, minced
- ❖ 3 garlic cloves, minced
- ❖ 1 small onion, minced

- ❖ 3/4 tsp cumin
- ❖ 1 1/2 tsp chili powder
- ❖ 4 Tbsp chopped fresh basil
- ❖ 4 Tbsp chopped fresh oregano
- ❖ Sea salt
- ❖ 3/4 cup vegetable stock

**How to Prepare**

1. Combine the quinoa and vegetable stock in a saucepan and place over medium high flame. Bring to a boil, then reduce to a simmer and cover. Cook for 30 minutes, or until liquid is completely absorbed by the quinoa. Set aside.

2. Set the oven to 400 degrees F.

3. Arrange the halved bell peppers on a baking sheet. Drizzle some olive oil over them, then season with salt and cayenne pepper. Turn to coat, and bake for 15 minutes, or until tender.

4. Meanwhile, place a large skillet over medium high flame and heat the olive oil. Saute the onion, garlic, carrot, celery, pumpkin seeds, chili powder, and cumin until vegetables are golden brown and tender.

5. Add the quinoa into the skillet, then fold in the basil. Saute until thoroughly combined, then season to taste with salt.

6. Lightly coat a casserole dish with olive oil and set aside.

7. Stuff the pepper halves with the filling, then arrange on the casserole dish. Pour the vegetable stock around the stuffed bell peppers, then cover the casserole dish with aluminum foil.

8. Bake for 25 minutes, then serve warm.

# Chapter 6 - Side Dishes

## *Roasted Squash with Herbs and Cranberries*

*Makes 3 servings*

### Ingredients

- ❖ 1 1/2 Tbsp canola oil

- ❖ 1 medium onion, sliced into wedges

- ❖ 1 medium butternut squash, peeled

- ❖ 1 tsp sea salt

- ❖ 1/4 tsp freshly ground black pepper

- ❖ 1/4 tsp ground nutmeg

- ❖ 1/4 tsp dried sage

- ❖ 1/4 cup dried cranberries

- ❖ Nonstick cooking spray

### How to Prepare

1. Set the oven to 400 degrees F. Lightly mist a baking sheet with nonstick cooking spray.

2. Halve the squash, then remove the seeds. Slice the squash into cubes and transfer to a bowl.

3. Drizzle the canola oil over the squash, then sprinkle with sage, nutmeg, black pepper, and salt. Add the onion and toss well to coat.

4. Spread the squash on a baking sheet in an even layer, then roast for 30 minutes, stirring every so often to prevent burning.

5. Remove the baking sheet from the oven and stir the cranberries in. Transfer to a platter and serve right away.

# Grilled Chinese Mustard Cabbage with Zesty Dressing

*Makes 6 servings*

## Ingredients

- ❖ 2 Tbsp toasted sesame oil

- ❖ 12 small heads Chinese mustard cabbage, roots trimmed

- ❖ 2/3 cup freshly squeezed orange juice

- ❖ 3 Tbsp tamari

- ❖ 2/3 tsp agave nectar

- ❖ Sea salt

- ❖ Freshly ground black pepper

## How to Prepare

1. Combine the orange juice, tamari, agave nectar, and 2/3 tablespoon of sesame oil. Set aside.

2. Prepare the stove top grill.

3. Place the Chinese mustard cabbage in a bowl and drizzle the remaining sesame oil on top. Toss to coat, then season with salt and pepper and toss again.

4. Grill the Chinese mustard cabbage for 3 minutes per side, then place on a serving plate.

5. Whisk the dressing again, then drizzle over the grilled Chinese mustard cabbage and serve right away.

# Toasted Sesame Kale

*Makes 6 servings*

## Ingredients

- ❖ 3 tsp olive oil
- ❖ 1 1/2 tsp toasted sesame oil
- ❖ 1 1/2 Tbsp sesame seeds
- ❖ 1 1/2 tsp minced garlic
- ❖ 1 1/2 Tbsp minced fresh ginger
- ❖ 3 bunches kale
- ❖ 1 1/2 Tbsp tamari

## How to Prepare

1. Chop the stems off the kale and mince. Shred the kale leaves and set aside.

2. Place a wok over medium flame and heat the sesame and olive oils together. Stir in the ginger and garlic for 1 minute, or until fragrant.

3. Stir in the chopped kale stems. Saute until tender, then stir in the chopped kale leaves and saute until wilted. Add a bit of water to prevent the kale from burning.

4. Add the sesame seeds and tamari and stir well until thoroughly combined. Transfer to a serving plate and serve right away.

# Steamed Broccoli with Spiced Molasses Dressing

*Makes 3 servings*

## Ingredients

- ❖ 1/2 tsp toasted sesame oil
- ❖ 3/4 lb fresh broccoli florets
- ❖ 1/4 tsp sea salt
- ❖ Freshly ground black pepper

*Dressing:*

- ❖ 1/4 cup vegetable stock
- ❖ 1/4 Tbsp cornstarch
- ❖ 1/4 Tbsp tamari
- ❖ 1 small garlic clove, minced
- ❖ 1/4 Tbsp molasses
- ❖ Ground ginger
- ❖ Crushed red pepper flakes

## How to Prepare

1. Combine the vegetable stock, tamari, cornstarch, and garlic in a saucepan. Stir in a

dash of ginger and red pepper flakes, then mix well.

2. Place over medium flame and let simmer, stirring frequently, until thickened. Reduce to low flame and add the molasses. Season to taste with salt and pepper, then set aside.

3. Boil some water in a nonstick skillet over high flame. Season with the salt and add the broccoli florets.

4. Cover and reduce to medium flame. Cook for 3 minutes, or until broccoli is tender. Transfer to a bowl and drizzle the sesame oil on top. Season with black pepper, then toss to coat.

5. Drizzle the dressing over the broccoli, then toss again to coat. Serve right away.

## *Humble Roasted Fennel*
*Makes 6 servings*

### Ingredients

- ❖ 1/4 cup olive oil
- ❖ 2 lemons
- ❖ 2 large fennel bulbs
- ❖ Sea salt
- ❖ Freshly ground black pepper

### How to Prepare

1. Set the oven to 375 degrees F. Coat a rimmed baking sheet with some of the olive oil and set aside.

2. Rinse the fennel bulbs thoroughly, then slice off the top ends. Place upright on a chopping board and slice into half inch pieces.

3. Arrange the sliced fennel in the prepared baking sheet, then drizzle the olive oil over them. Season with salt and pepper, then toss to coat.

4. Spread out the fennel slices in an even layer, then roast for 20 minutes.

5. Turn over the fennel slices, then roast for an additional 20 minutes.

6. Remove the baking sheet and place on a cooling rack. Halve the lemons and squeeze the juice all over the roasted fennel. Serve right away.

# Minty Crisp Red Beans

*Makes 2 servings*

## Ingredients

- ❖ 2 Tbsp peanut oil
- ❖ 8 oz canned red beans, rinsed and drained thoroughly
- ❖ 1 1/2 Tbsp whole wheat flour
- ❖ 1/4 cup chopped fresh mint
- ❖ Sea salt
- ❖ Freshly ground black pepper
- ❖ Cayenne pepper

## How to Prepare

1. Season the flour with a dash of cayenne and salt. Mix well.

2. Blot the red beans dry with paper towels, then add to the flour and toss until thoroughly coated.

3. Cover a platter with paper towels, then set aside.

4. Place a wok over medium high flame and heat the oil. Carefully stir in the beans and stir fry until golden and crisp.

5. Move the beans to the prepared platter using a slotted spoon. Let drain, then transfer to a serving plate and fold in the mint. Serve right away.

## *Spicy Oriental Greens*

*Makes 3 servings*

### Ingredients

- ❖ 4 cups chopped Napa cabbage, rinsed and drained thoroughly
- ❖ 4 cups chopped red chard, rinsed and drained thoroughly
- ❖ 4 cups chopped green chard, rinsed and drained thoroughly

*Dressing:*

- ❖ 1/2 tsp minced garlic cloves
- ❖ 1 scallion, chopped
- ❖ 1 tsp pure maple syrup
- ❖ 1/3 tsp crushed red chili flakes
- ❖ 1 1/4 Tbsp chopped fresh cilantro
- ❖ 3/4 Tbsp freshly squeezed lime juice
- ❖ 2 Tbsp tamari
- ❖ 1 Tbsp canola oil
- ❖ 1 Tbsp toasted sesame oil
- ❖ 1/2 Tbsp grated fresh ginger

- ❖ 1 Tbsp white sesame seeds

- ❖ 1 Tbsp black sesame seeds

## How to Prepare

1. In a bowl, combine the canola oil, sesame oil, tamari, sesame seeds, garlic, cilantro, maple syrup, red chili flakes, scallions, ginger, and lime juice.

2. Boil 4 cups of water in a saucepan, then add the Napa cabbage and chard. Cook for 30 seconds or until wilted, then immediately drain in a steel colander.

3. Transfer the greens into a bowl, then pour the sauce evenly on top. Toss well to coat, then serve right away.

# Okra Masala

*Makes 2 servings*

## Ingredients

- ❖ 1 Tbsp canola or olive oil
- ❖ 1/2 lb fresh okra, trimmed and sliced
- ❖ 1/2 yellow onion, peeled and minced
- ❖ 2 small garlic cloves, minced
- ❖ 1/4 tsp cayenne pepper
- ❖ 1/2 tsp turmeric
- ❖ 1 tsp garam masala
- ❖ 1/4 tsp cinnamon
- ❖ 1/2 tsp sea salt
- ❖ 1/2 tsp black mustard seeds
- ❖ 2 Tbsp vegetable stock
- ❖ 1/2 Tbsp freshly squeezed lime juice
- ❖ 1/2 cup diced tomatoes

## How to Prepare

1. Place a wok over high flame and heat the oil. Stir in the mustard seeds and place a lid over

the wok. Shake the wok slightly until the seeds pop.

2. Remove the lid and add the garlic. Sauté for 5 seconds, then stir in the onion and sauté until onion is translucent.

3. Add the okra and stir fry for 2 minutes. Stir in the spices and salt, then stir fry for 1 minute.

4. Add the vegetable broth and cover the wok once more. Reduce to medium high flame and cook for 8 minutes, stirring occasionally. Add a bit more broth occasionally to prevent drying out.

5. Add the tomatoes and lime juice and stir well for 2 minutes. Transfer to a plate and serve right away.

# Spiced Crisp Cauliflower
*Makes 2 servings*

## Ingredients

- ❖ 2 Tbsp canola oil
- ❖ 3 cups chopped cauliflower florets
- ❖ 1/4 cup frozen peas, thawed
- ❖ 1/2 cup minced red onion
- ❖ 1/2 tsp minced garlic
- ❖ 1/4 tsp fennel seeds
- ❖ 1/2 Tbsp freshly grated ginger
- ❖ 1/4 tsp garam masala
- ❖ 1/4 tsp curry powder
- ❖ 1/8 tsp crushed red chili flakes
- ❖ 1/4 Tbsp freshly grated lemon zest
- ❖ 1 tsp sea salt
- ❖ 1/2 tsp freshly ground black pepper
- ❖ 2 Tbsp chopped fresh cilantro
- ❖ Nonstick cooking spray

## How to Prepare

1. Set the oven to 400 degrees F. Lightly coat a rimmed baking sheet with nonstick cooking spray and set aside.

2. In a mixing bowl, combine the canola oil, cauliflower, lemon zest, black pepper, salt, garam masala, curry powder, red chili flakes, fennel seeds, ginger, garlic, and onion. Toss well.

3. Spread the cauliflower mixture on the prepared rimmed baking sheet and roast for 15 to 20 minutes, or until the cauliflower is golden brown and crisp.

4. Add the thawed peas into the mixture and toss well with the roasted cauliflower to warm through.

5. Transfer the roasted cauliflower mixture onto a serving platter, sprinkle the cilantro on top, then serve right away.

# Spicy Asian Eggplant

*Makes 2 servings*

## Ingredients

- ❖  2 large Asian eggplants

- ❖  4 garlic cloves, minced

- ❖  1 1/2 Tbsp canola oil

- ❖  1 1/2 Tbsp toban djan bean sauce

- ❖  1 Tbsp tamari

- ❖  1 1/2 Tbsp rice vinegar

- ❖  1 tsp agave nectar

- ❖  2 Tbsp water

- ❖  1 tsp cornstarch

- ❖  3 green onions, green part, sliced

## How to Prepare

1. Slice eggplants into 3 inch pieces, then halve each piece. Set aside.

2. Place a wok over medium high flame and heat 1 tablespoon of canola oil. Stir in the eggplant and stir-fry until tender. Transfer to a plate lined with paper towels and set aside.

3. Heat the remaining canola oil in the wok, then stir in the garlic and toban djan bean sauce. Stir in the rice vinegar, agave nectar, and tamari, mixing well.

4. Return the eggplant into the wok and stir fry to heat through and mix with the sauce.

5. Place a lid over the wok and cook over medium low flame for 3 minutes.

6. Add 2 tablespoons of water and stir fry for 2 minutes, or until eggplant is very tender.

7. Combine the cornstarch and water in a small bowl, then pour into the wok. Stir fry until the sauce becomes thick.

8. Transfer the mixture onto a platter and sprinkle the green onion on top. Serve right away.

# Conclusion

In this book you have learned how to prepare easy and affordable dishes that fit into the whole food plant based diet. Stay inspired and motivated to follow this diet so that you can fulfill your goals and enjoy living life to the fullest with a healthy body and mind.

While this diet does require dedication and perseverance, all the health benefits that come with it are definitely worth the effort.

Made in the USA
Lexington, KY
26 January 2017